TRAMCAR
STOCK B

Compiled by
John Senior and Ian Stewart

TRAMCAR ROLLING STOCK BOOK

© 2007 Venture Publications Ltd

ISBN 978 1 905304 202

The Editors and Publisher thank those who have provided additional photographs
to fill gaps which otherwise would have existed in the coverage of this work.
Their contributions are listed on the rear inside cover.

DESIGN & COMPUTER ORIGINATION: JOHN A SENIOR

The activity at Town End, the lower terminus, always attracts curious onlookers.

CONTENTS

After climbing to the top of the line trams reverse at this high point.

FRONTISPIECE

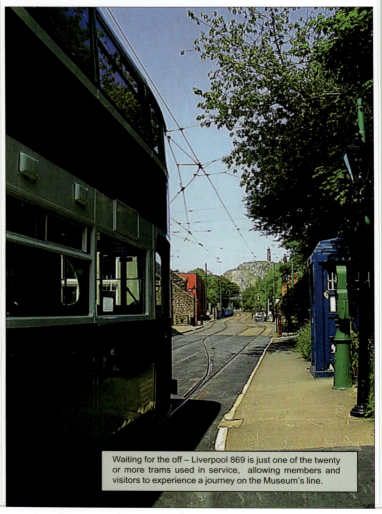

Waiting for the off – Liverpool 869 is just one of the twenty or more trams used in service, allowing members and visitors to experience a journey on the Museum's line.

FOREWORD

"Great Oaks from little acorns grow"

The Oxford Dictionary of Quotations attributes this to being a 14th century proverb but it certainly describes the evolution of the National Tramway Museum. For those who have not been part of its development over the past fifty years it might be hard to picture the almost surreal image of a misty, deserted quarry and abandoned narrow gauge railway that served it as a reminder of times past. This was what a small band of local Tramway Museum Society members stumbled across when looking for a home for a single tram (Sheffield 189).

The Society emerged in 1955 from a determined, single-minded group that had originally been part of the Light Railway Transport League. They inherited a small number of deteriorating relics but had nowhere to protect them from everything that the weather and growing vandalism could throw at them, and not all survived for posterity. Out of this has grown the Crich Tramway Museum of today. Once this home had been found, those pioneers were spurred on by their ambition and vision for greater times ahead. The movement has been variously described as "The Tramway Museum Society", "The TMS", or, simply "The Society", operating "The Museum" or ""The Tramway Museum". All these descriptions are used in this book without apology. However, it was not long before what had originally been known as "the site" was being called "The National Tramway Museum".

This led some sceptics to question how the Collection and facilities could possibly be put on a par with the National *Railway* Museum at York. And yet, and yet. Look around and you see that this is exactly what did happen. It is not for nothing that the Museum was given 'Designated Status', a mark of recognition in the Museum world which records its high standing. Not for nothing that its restoration work and conservation policies are seen by professionals here and abroad to be the benchmark for others to achieve.

It simply ranks among the top in the world. Of course, the nucleus of the Museum is the fleet of trams which are its very raison d'etre. They are here in this Stock Book to be studied, savoured and admired. Many are testament to municipal pride but they are also a tribute not only to their original builders but particularly to those who have painstakingly restored them and keep them running.

INTRODUCTION

The collection of trams at the National Tramway Museum now contains over 50 examples; many are in full working order, others are static exhibition items, others are awaiting restoration and some are in store. A selection from the working fleet operates each day that the Museum is open, giving visitors the opportunity to sample the different types of trams in the collection, and, often, to ride on a tram from their own home town – a real opportunity to turn the clock back.

Many people will never have ridden on a tram in this country, though they may have done so when on holiday abroad. For them, and the many younger people who visit the Museum, we hope that this will be an experience that they will savour. All our trams run on standard gauge track, where the rails are 4'-8½" apart, and with the exception of the horse trams, the steam tram trailer and some members of our engineering fleet, draw their electric current from the overhead wires. One, Howth 10, was originally built to run on the Irish broad gauge of 5'-3" whilst all the Glasgow trams have been regauged from their native city's 4'-7¾" gauge to our standard. The Sheffield Works car No.330 originally ran in Bradford and, with the Derby car No.1, were formerly 4'-0" gauge cars and there is also on display one bogie from the Snaefell Mountain Railway with its 3'-6" gauge. If 4'-8½" was "standard", it was not universal.

The overhead line carries 600Volts and this power is supplied from the national grid through our own substation. The electricity returns through the

rails, as it did and still does on surviving tramways, and the rails have mostly been recovered from defunct systems throughout the country. Once again the work of laying the track and maintaining it falls in the main to our own volunteers, though in more recent times some work has been contracted out to specialist firms, thus easing the load on our small but dedicated workforce.

The vehicles span a period which saw immense change. The oldest, Oporto 9, dates from 1873 whilst the newest, Halle 902, was built in 1969. Their design illustrates the evolution of the tram, and its ability to adapt to varying requirements, providing everyday transport in major cities, large and small towns, seaside resorts and even along a cliff-side line in the Isle of Man.

Whilst the majority come from England and Scotland, in addition to the Manx car we have one Welsh tram from Cardiff and one Irish example from the Hill of Howth line, already mentioned, and originally owned by the Great Northern Railway of Ireland, in whose colours it can be seen in the Exhibition Hall. Examples from further afield have been brought to Crich from Austria, Belgium, Czechoslovakia, Germany, The Netherlands, Portugal and South Africa, whilst our steam tram aka *John Bull* spent its early life in Australia. Future additions may perhaps see this list extended.

The Museum's policy is to build a collection which shows the development of the tram as a prime mover of people, and although we have over 50 examples there are still some significant gaps. For many years there was no representative of the ubiquitous four-wheel balcony car which was so much

a part of almost every British town, except for the Johannesburg car which was at least built in Preston, Lancashire. In 1972 the restoration by volunteers of Leicester 76, now honorably retired into the Exhibition Hall, was completed, and 25 years later in 1997 the Museum workshop finished the recreation of Chesterfield 7 from a former holiday home at a cost of over £250,000. Other gaps have been covered by such rebuilding of former summerhouses or holiday homes whilst, in other cases, trams have been taken back to their earlier condition as in the case of Paisley 68 as an open-topper, but recreating the past is a hugely expensive task as the Chesterfield exercise demonstrates.

Much of the work was carried out by enthusiasts working in their spare time, often away from the Museum, and when their labours were finished the end result was proudly brought to the Museum. Others have been rebuilt or completely restored in our own workshop and from the new viewing gallery it is possible to see some of this work being accomplished. The workshop employs a full-time painter and signwriter whose work instantly catches the eye on these wonderful vehicles. Equally vital work encompasses the regular servicing, maintenance, and cleaning of the operational trams.

Just as important as the turnout of the trams is that of their crews, and all the smartly uniformed inspectors, drivers and conductors have been fully trained by the Museum's own instructors. There are many types of control gear on the different trams, and drivers have to be competent, assessed, and passed to drive, each type of car which they will be rostered to operate in service. Similarly, conductors are taught the art of looking after passengers, something lost in this age of one-person-operation in most public transport. They are, though, spared such chores as dealing with money and changing ten-shilling notes for penny fares – once the bane of their predecessor's lives – since the tram rides are free on presentation of the pre-decimal penny issued when visitors enter the Museum.

This booklet gives details of the operating fleet, the non-operational cars in the Exhibition Hall, together with some of the visitors, works cars and items in store or operating away from Crich. Even now there are trams waiting to come to the Museum and there will always be something new to experience with each visit there. Long may it be so!

A SURVEY OF THE PASSENGER CARS

Leeds 602, the most modern British-built example in the collection, dating from 1953 and sporting its Royal Purple livery to celebrate the Queen's Coronation that year, pauses to pick up passengers before continuing up the line to the terminus, giving panoramic views across the picturesque Derwent valley below on the left as it does so.

The wide selection of vehicles in the collection allows visitors and enthusiasts alike to experience riding on trams old and new, built for differing work loads and environments, but, above all, doing just what they were designed for all those years ago!

DERBY 1

In the early years of the Museum's existence it soon became apparent that visitors wanted to see a tram from their home town. Derby was an obvious choice for such a vehicle, with many people coming to Crich from that nearby town. The body of this tram had been a holiday home at Mickleover from 1932, a fate which befell many trams when withdrawn from service at that time, and much time and effort went into finding and installing missing components, including the all-important staircases.

The four-wheel truck on which the body sits came from Blackpool's illuminated 'Gondola' car, itself originally number 28, a former Marton 'box' car which was broken up at Crich. The finished result enhances the Exhibition Hall, catching the eye of many from its home town who remember the pleasing livery as soon as they enter the Hall. It is not operational, and has never run. It is a typical British 3-window car of a type to be found operating throughout the British Isles, a product of the Edwardian tram building boom years.

The display is intended to replicate a typical exhibit as it would have been presented to visitors to a Tramway and Light Railway Exhibition of that period, and a suitable taped commentary adds to the atmosphere.

DOUGLAS SOUTHERN ELECTRIC 1

One of the most remarkable survivors in the collection is this tram, seen here as it was operating until 1939 when wartime constraints caused the closure of its system which ran between Douglas and Port Soderick in the Isle of Man. It remained in the depot with its fellows, undisturbed, until rescued in 1951. Dating from 1896, it features American equipment, the most significant of which is probably the Lord Baltimore truck, and is unusual in being equipped for operation on a line where passengers were picked up on one side only due to the proximity of the cliff face on the landward side.

Never restored, ownership of the car was passed to the British Transport Commission (BTC) when they agreed to look after it. When the National Railway Museum was set up at York, ownership passed to the Science Museum and during Sir Neil Cossons' period as Director of that latter institution that the Tramway Museum Society was able to use his good offices to have ownership of the car transferred to, and included within, the collection at Crich. The car runs very occasionally but is normally a static exhibit due to its pioneering mechanical and electrical equipment being irreplaceable.

LONDON COUNTY COUNCIL 1

When the London Passenger Transport Board (LPTB) was formed in 1933 it inherited a wide selection of trams of varying pedigrees, capabilities and vintages. The London County Council (LCC) had produced a protoype for the new organisation, being numbered 1, and embodying the latest features from the tramcar industry. More conservative in appearance than the innovative Feltham trams recently introduced by the Underground Group, this LCC swansong was in many ways a more practical operating vehicle. It entered service in a special royal blue and white livery, and traces of this can be seen to this day where the London Transport red paint has cracked. Trams did not figure in London Transport's vision for the future, so No.1 became a 'one-off'. It was not popular with motormen unfamiliar with its controls, seeing less service than it deserved. It was sold to Leeds Corporation in 1951, becoming their No.301, as seen, and this ensured its survival.

Its importance lies in it being the antecedent of the Liverpool 'Robinson' cars based to a large extent on drawings of No.1 supplied from London. These paved the way for further Liverpool modern cars such as the 'Liners', like 869 at Crich, and the modern Glasgow Coronation cars such as 1282, also at Crich.

LCC No.1, as Leeds 301, was housed at the BTC Clapham Museum, in London, and when that collection was dispersed, the car came to Crich where it has received a cosmetic, London Transport, repaint for display purposes pending a full and costly planned restoration.

BLACKPOOL & FLEETWOOD 2

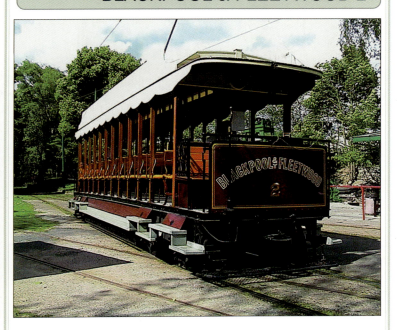

This roofed toastrack tram was built in 1898 by the GF Milnes company of Birkenhead, and was operated by the privately-owned Blackpool & Fleetwood Tramroad Company from its Bispham depot until Blackpool Corporation purchased the Tramroad Company in 1920, when the rolling stock passed into its ownership. The company cars were gradually withdrawn when Blackpool modernised its fleet in the 'thirties but this car survived to be restored for the 75th Anniversary of tramcar operation in the Borough in 1960. It came to Crich in 1963, and has been a regular and always very popular performer since then.

In 1998 it returned to Blackpool for the celebrations to commemorate the Centenary of the Blackpool & Fleetwood Tramroad, and returned to Crich later that year. Always popular with visitors it is similar to cars still operating in the Isle of Man, and indeed the Manager of the Blackpool Company was also Manager of the Manx Electric Railway at that time.

BLACKPOOL CONDUIT CAR '1'

When Blackpool began tramway operation in 1885 its pioneers used a system of conduit collection to feed electricity to the tramcar's motor. A slot in a centre rail gave access to the live rail below ground, with current return via the running rails. This system was plagued by problems with sand and sea water being blown onto the roadway, and dropping through the slot, hampering the passage of current. In 1899 overhead wires were installed and the troublesome conduit system was abandoned. Among the original rolling stock were two small cars, including the surviving No.4, constructed by the Lancaster Carriage & Wagon Company. Its survival is all the more remarkable when it is considered that it was withdrawn from passenger service as long ago as 1912, having long since acquired a more conventional truck. During the First World War No. 4 was put to use delivering bread to the military camp established at Squires Gate. For this purpose it was fitted with a pair of side doors. When no longer required for these duties it was equipped with an overhead inspection tower and survived in this form until 1934 when it was stored out of use.

It lay at the back of Bispham Depot until it was driven to the Rigby Road Works early in 1960 to be restored for the Celebrations marking the 75th Anniversary of the start of operation in Blackpool, claiming (wrongly) to be the original number 1 as seen above. Unlike the other trams restored for this event, the car was not allowed to carry members of the public, probably

on account of its fragility. Shortly afterwards it was donated to the TMS and loaned by the Society to the BTC, to join a collection of transport vehicles stored, and later displayed, in the former Clapham tram depot in London.

In 1984 it was restored again and given replica running gear, similar in appearance and operation to its original equipment. This included a 4hp electric motor powered by rechargeable batteries, and was complete with suitable (modern) control gear. The 1960 red and white livery was replaced by a more accurate representation of the original sage green and gamboge with large and distinctive numerals confirming its correct identity as '4' on each dash.

It operated successfully in Blackpool for the Centenary in 1985, subsequently spending some time at the Manchester Museum of Science & Technology, before returning to Crich. It is rarely seen in service, spending most of its time on display in the entrance to the Exhibition Hall but makes appearances for special occasions such as the 50th Anniversary of the hand-over of the Society's very first tram, number 45, re-enacted on 29th May 2005, exactly fifty years to the day. Number 4 is illustrated participating in this event, suitably decorated in traditional manner.

GATESHEAD 5

As with many of the exhibits, number 5's journey to Crich was not straightforward, as will be seen. The car was constructed in the Sunderland Road workshops of the Gateshead & District Tramways in 1927. Low bridges dictated that double-deckers were not the Company's first choice, hence the need for a long single-decker to gain equivalent capacity. The roof features a rather splendid clerestory with ruby glass quarterlights although concealed from view by advert boards. The reversed maximum traction bogies have 32in diameter wheels, and clearance for these gives passengers a commanding view of pedestrians. Number 5 is very definitely *not* a 'low-floor, easy access' tram!

The Gateshead operation was the last tramway operated by British Electric Traction (BET), closing in 1951. British Railways purchased 19 cars for their Grimsby & Immingham Tramway to augment the former Great Central Railway fleet (like No.14 at Crich). The line closed in 1961 but ensured that their No.20 survived to be restored as Gateshead number 5, arriving at Crich in March 1963. The car has been restored in several stages from 1967 and was intended for operation at the 1990 Gateshead Garden Festival to which it was despatched but not operated due to difficulties with the track there. It was exchanged for Blackpool 167 and operated at Crich for the 1990 season, achieving the highest mileage of all operating trams in that year.

Although popular with visitors, open-top trams are not always compatible with Crich weather, as can be seen above, and cars such as No. 5 then come into their own – to the relief of all concerned!

In the ever-more difficult times for Blackpool Corporation Transport during the 1970s it became increasingly obvious that operation of 48-seat Railcoaches with conductors was quite uneconomical. Operation of one-man buses with higher capacities had proved to be feasible, and thirteen of the English Electric Railcoaches were converted for this use. The modifications were quite extensive, involving lengthening of the bodywork from 43 to 49ft, and creation of front entrances to the motorman's left where fares could be collected. To signify to passengers that they would not be assisted by conductors, and should have the exact fare to hand when boarding, the trams were given a special 'plum & custard' livery, later red and ivory and finally in variations of the normal green and cream. They were renumbered in the series 1-13 and are generally recognised as saving the tramway by giving it a stay of execution until new trams became available, from 1984.

Intensively used, the added end-weight caused the bodywork to distort on several cars and the last was withdrawn after the 1991 season. Number 5 had a Brecknell Willis single arm pantograph for a while before acquiring a more conventional example. After carrying the red and ivory livery it latterly carried the more normal fleet livery. It was set aside for the TMS and is currently in store at Clay Cross, ultimately to represent the transitional stage between the first and second generation tramways.

CHESTERFIELD 7

Number 7 is one of the original twelve open-top trams purchased from the Brush Company of Loughborough for the opening of the electrified Chesterfield system in 1904. The body is four-window type, with open balconies to the upper-deck, the car having originally been open-topped.

When the opportunity arose to recreate No. 7, once retrieved from the Derbyshire moors at Darley Dale where it had resided since 1927, another local tram joined the collection. This time, however, the resources were available to make the car a working exhibit and after many years in storage, the parts were collected, copied if necessary, and assembled into a working exhibit whereby it is now a regular performer on the Museum line. Despite prolonged exposure, some of the panelling still had traces of the original livery that was carefully reproduced to ensure accuracy of the painting style.

The work of rebuilding the tram was carried out in the Museum's own workshop, taking over two years. It is always a favourite with visitors and the eye-catching livery of chocolate and primrose undoubtedly adds to its popularity. The truck was salvaged from Sheffield Corporation's No.349 whose last duties had been as an illuminated car during the final weeks before closure. That car became better known as '01' at Crich following its rebuilding as the Museum's first generator car, as seen on page 95.

Given the pace of electrification of horse tramway systems around the end of the 19th century, Chesterfield number 8 was a late entrant to service in 1899, by which time many undertakings had already taken their decisions to electrify their systems. The comparatively large windows are a clue to its vintage, anticipating designs that had yet to appear on electric trams. The style should be contrasted with the design of Oporto horse car number 9 on the following page. Number 8 was constructed by GF Milnes as a 16-seater but only had a short service life, being withdrawn in 1904, and then sold to become yet another summerhouse when Chesterfield's only route from Brampton to Whittington was electrified. It was eventually rescued and restored by Chesterfield's own Transport Department and found its way to the erstwhile BTC collection at Clapham, already mentioned.

Another victim of the dispersal of their tramway exhibits, number 8 went into storage during which time ineffective weatherproofing caused unwanted damage that had to be put right. When this was done, the opportunity was taken to apply the correct livery and the car participated in its home town's Transport Centenary in 1982. Later that year the car came to Crich where it has on occasion been joined by buses from the Chesterfield undertaking. It remains on long-term loan from the National Museum of Science and Industry in London and performs for special events, as shown above.

OPORTO 9

This 16-seater was built by the Starbuck Car & Wagon Company and is the oldest exhibit in the collection. As a trailer car from Portugal, it is the only one that has been hauled by three different forms of traction comprising mules, steam and electricity. It dates from 1873 and was in continuous service until 1960, retaining some of the features found in the very first trams introduced to this country by George Francis Train in 1860. The round-topped windows are typical of the earliest trams in Birkenhead, and could also be seen in examples running in Govan and Glasgow in the 1870s.

Following withdrawal, number 9 was repainted but saw only occasional use before acquisition by the TMS for shipping back to England. It arrived at Crich in 1964 having had the transportation costs sponsored by Sandeman's Port. It used to be the regular trailer for steam locomotive *John Bull* and has since been repainted in original livery with enormous numerals '9' on each dash for the short sighted.

Built for the Irish Hill of Howth line, this tram was owned by the Great Northern Railway of Ireland, in whose distinctive varnished teak livery it is preserved. Originally operating on the Irish 5ft 3in broad gauge, it was regauged standard gauge to allow it to take part in the Blackpool Centenary celebrations . Prone to derailing in its original form, its performance was improved by a modification to the bogies during its last few years of operation. The Howth line operated with ten cars (plus a works car) but the derailing problems ensured that numbers 9 and 10 led a sheltered life, while the brunt of the service was carried by more conventional cars 1-8. This explains number 10's almost 'as new' condition for a 1902 tram.The seating in the lower-deck is unusual, being back-to-back longitudinal down the centre of the saloon, reflecting the attractive nature of the line and the splendid views to be seen from the tram.

In 1985 it joined other trams from Crich to operate in Blackpool during the celebration of the Centenary of electric tramway operation in the Borough, the first such in the British Isles. It had been brought back to operating condition at Smithills workshops in Bolton before going to the coast, and returned to Crich when the celebrations finished. It will normally be found in the Exhibition Hall, as seen here.

GRIMSBY & IMMINGHAM 14

Grimsby & Immingham number 14 has a few claims to being unique among the Crich Collection. At over 54ft it is the longest, and takes up as much depot space as two small four wheelers. It is also the only tram formerly owned by a UK railway company. It was originally built by the Great Central Railway in 1915 at their Dukinfield Works, acquired by the LNER in the1923 amalgamation and then, following nationalisation, passed to British Railways whose green livery and 'starved lion' emblem it now carries. It also has the highest seating capacity of any single-decker, accommodating 72.

Number 14's line was constructed to handle major traffic flows of dock workers between Grimsby town and the then new Immingham Dock. In some respects it resembled the Blackpool and Fleetwood Tramroad in being a mixture of tramway and railway practice. Perhaps this explains its subsequent travels since the line closed in 1961. Number 14 never joined the other trams at the BTC Museum in Clapham. It actually made the trip to the National Railway Museum in York in 1989 after some years stored with other BR relics at Clay Cross. After standing outside at York, it came back to Derbyshire in 1990 joining the collection at Crich where it has been repainted in the livery carried by Gateshead No.5 when it first arrived at the Museum as Grimsby & Immingham No.20.

SHEFFIELD CORPORATION 15

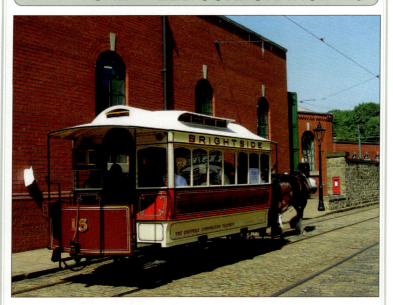

One of the early arrivals at the Museum in 1959, this tram's first life finished after it was withdrawn from passenger service in 1902. It was then used in Sheffield as an emergency (or works) car for many years after the body was fitted onto an electric truck. During this time it was renumbered 166 in the electric fleet. Following restoration of running gear at Crich it later returned to Sheffield to allow it to form part of the Christmas festivities in 1962. Whilst at Sheffield the Transport Department repainted the car in the early Sheffield 'red' livery. It was operated in passenger service briefly during 1963, using a very short stretch of the first main line which society members had then laid. By the following year electric trams would be operating at Crich.

Used only on high days and holidays, with appropriate 'motive-power', it allows visitors of all ages to experience a form of transport which disappeared from most towns and cities in this country before the First Word War, though happily horse trams continue to operate in the Isle of Man, on 3ft gauge tracks, taking holiday-makers along the famous Douglas promenade for several months each year.

DUNDEE & DISTRICT 21

Steam trams, which took the place of horse trams in many towns, were capable of hauling large capacity double-deck trailers, and this former Dundee example has been painstakingly restored to its original condition to provide an example for the collection. The body is noteworthy for being fully enclosed, apart from the staircases, despite being built in 1894 by GF Milnes for the Company, for whom it ran until 1902 before being taken over by Dundee Corporation. It would not be until some 25 years later that electric trams were able to offer this degree of protection from the elements, though balcony top covers such as that fitted to Chesterfield 7, seen previously, were a first step in that direction.

Steam tram trailers needed to be covered to keep smoke and cinders from the engines from dropping onto the top deck passengers. Although complete in most respects, number 21 is not operational. Like some other exhibits its restoration was finished at Smithills, Bolton, as part of a youth training scheme in the 1980s, and it now forms part of the static display in the Exhibition Hall.

Fate played its part in the preservation of various Glasgow trams in the Collection, as will be seen. Number 22 was not destined for preservation at all. Car 108 had been selected and but for its destruction in the Dalmarnock depot fire of 1961, would probably be running today at Crich with Red Route colour livery (like 1115, page 71). Number 22 was at Maryhill depot, performing shunting duties by that time, and stepped into the limelight as a second choice from the dwindling number of Glasgow Standard trams.

The car was taken to the Coplawhill Car Works, restored to its original 1922 open-balcony condition, and repainted with White Route colour, arriving at Crich in 1963, the year following the Glasgow closure. It was one of the first exhibits to do so in anything like a restored condition. But there was much still to do, and the car has received several major overhauls since, including a re-fit to allow it to run at the 1988 Glasgow Garden Festival where it became the VIP tram. As such it conveyed the Prince & Princess of Wales, The Princess Royal and Prince Philip, not forgetting the 'Iron Lady' herself, Margaret Thatcher, and her husband Denis. It ran faultlessly for the 152 days of intensive operation and covered over 4,000 miles. On returning to Crich it went straight back into service, none the worse for its adventure.

EDINBURGH 35

Another unlikely survivor, City & Royal Burgh of Edinburgh number 35 (to give the full title) was a substitute for 225 when it had been involved in a serious accident two months before abandonment of the system in 1956. One of 84 domed roof Standard cars constructed at the Shrubhill Works from 1934 onwards to replace the remaining former cable cars, 35 was one of the last, being outshopped for service in 1948 – and became a fine example of a traditional, neat and well-proportioned British double-decker.

Thus 35 was to have a short working life in the Scottish Capital, but was set aside for preservation, initially being displayed in a small Museum within the Shrubhill Works. When that closed it languished for a few years before being sent to Blackpool in 1983 where it participated in the tramway Centenary celebrations in 1985, staying until 1988 when it returned to Scotland to operate at the Glasgow Garden Festival, sponsored by British Gas. At the end of that event, 35 came to Crich where it can usually be seen in the Exhibition Hall awaiting a major overhaul before joining the running fleet.

It is seen coming down from the top section of the Crich line at the point where the replica lead mine display is situated. See also page 88.

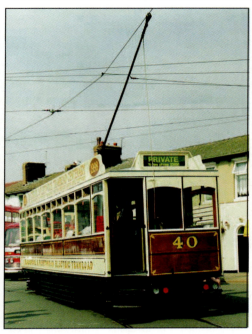

Blackpool Corporation took over the Blackpool & Fleetwood Tramroad Company in 1920 and thus acquired an additional 41 cars. Number 40 was the second newest, having been built in 1914 by the United Electric Car Company based in Preston. Renumbered 114 by its new owners, it continued to operate on the Fleetwood service despite relegation by the new Pantograph cars (like 167, page 48). When they, in turn, were cascaded by the new Railcoaches, 114's sorties became ever more spasmodic until withdrawal from service in 1939.

Subsequently renumbered '5' in the engineering fleet, and initially stabled at Copse Road depot, Fleetwood, it latterly resided at Rigby Road when acquired by the Overhead Department.

Its glory days came when it was restored as '40' again for the Tramway's 75th Anniversary. It was one of the restored cars offered to the TMS, and in1963 it duly arrived at Crich where it has always been known as 'Box 40' to distinguish it from 'Balcony 40' (page 28). It was one of the first operational cars at Crich but was withdrawn needing major mechanical and bodywork repairs. It went to Heaton Park, Manchester, to have this done in time for a return to Blackpool for their 1985 Centenary celebrations. It was a regular performer in the Park for some years. Returning to Clay Cross for storage in 1991, it was back on home metals again in 1996 participating in the Centenary of the Tramroad in 1998.

BLACKPOOL BALCONY 40

From the mid-1920s until the advent of the modern Railcoach influx the mainstay of the Blackpool fleet were the large, traditional Standard trams of which there were 42. Like Glasgow's Standard trams, they were judiciously improved over the years, all acquiring enclosed platforms and 17 (like number 49, page 32) were totally enclosed before the advent of World War II. The Railcoach fleet cascaded the Standards to the inland Marton route and for seasonal extras. Again, like the Glasgow Standards, they were a long time in departing the scene and the last was not withdrawn from normal passenger use until 1966.

Number 40 was the last open balcony Standard in Blackpool and the last to operate in the UK. Its significance was recognised and it was another of the historic cars offered to the TMS in 1962, duly arriving at Crich in 1963. It was within the nucleus of trams providing the initial running fleet and operated in the Blackpool green and cream livery in which it arrived, such was its excellent condition at the time. This livery styling had superseded the original red, white and teak style around 1933 and was one of the innovations of the visionary General Manager, Walter Luff, who persevered with trams when others did not, and invested in the fleet of new Railcoaches and streamlined trams, many of which have exceeded 70 years in service.

In 1983 Balcony 40 became due for a major overhaul at Crich, and it was decided that when the work was complete the car should be returned to the red and teak livery of the later 1920s which it carried when first outshopped in this form, and as shown here. The car is one of the regular performers and its high capacity and open balconies make it a useful vehicle for moving large parties, with fresh air for those who wish to sit in the open.

Built with handbrakes only for normal use, the tram provides an interesting example of how an efficent braking system, dependent only on the strength of the driver's arm, can cope with a large and, when loaded, heavy tram. It incorporates an electric brake, of course, but this would be used only in emergency. It returned to Blackpool in 1985 and became part of the iconic logo for the 'Blackpool 100' celebrations in that year. It is a typical Lancashire tram of its period.

SOUTHAMPTON 45

The first tram in the Museum's collection, and as such the most famous. Rescued by several enthusiasts after a tour of Southampton on a similar car in 1948, and purchased fully repainted and with a reconditioned truck under the body for the princely sum of £10, the tram became the possession of the group which formed the Society later in 1955. The tram was built to pass beneath the medieval Bargate in its home town, and its low height was achieved in several ways.

Most noticeable is the way in which the lower saloon ceiling projects upwards into the 'knifeboard' seating of the top deck. The impressive timber construction of the lower deck roof is worthy of note, as also is the warning notice painted on the panels above the stairs warning passengers of the dangers of touching the overhead wires.

Stored in Leeds, Blackpool, and then displayed at the Montagu Motor Museum in Beaulieu, Hampshire, before coming to Crich in October 1960, the car is always in great demand on warm sunny days.

SHEFFIELD 46

Sheffield is a hilly city and the severity of gradients and curves on such as those to Walkley and Intake precluded the use of double-deck trams in the system's early years. This accounts for there being a need for no less than 69 single-deckers. Number 46 was one of them, built in 1899 by GF Milnes, part of an order for twelve cars. By 1918 braking systems were seen to be sufficiently reliable to permit double-deckers to run safely on these routes. Some single-deckers were converted to double-deck configuration, some were sold to no less than seven other undertakings. Twelve were converted as snowploughs, including No. 46 which acquired new numbers 97 and 275 before finally becoming '354' in the departmental fleet. Vestibules were fitted in 1940 and the centre window of the five window saloon was taken out to shorten the car. Number 354 survived until 1960 to be restored to passenger condition by local TMS members and given back its old number before running in the closing procession for the Sheffield tramways.

On arrival at Crich it became one of the early operational fleet and despite some major work to eliminate the effects of salt corrosion, it is now stored off site at Clay Cross, hopefully awaiting its turn for a major restoration – to original 5-window condition?

BLACKPOOL STANDARD 49

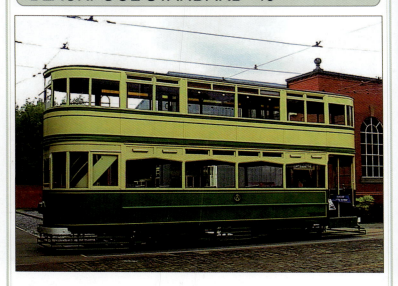

A later development of the Blackpool Standard car upgrading from the status of Balcony 40, (pages 28 & 29) with the upper-deck completely enclosed in 1938. This time the tram is made up of two parts. The lower-deck was constructed in 1926 but the upper-deck was salvaged from a much older 'Motherwell' car of 1902 vintage that had short saloons which created longer open ends. The partitions that formed these can be seen clearly in the illustration. Displaced from mainstream Promenade duties, the Standards operated on inland routes and as seasonal extras. Their numbers dwindled and No.49 was withdrawn in 1962, arriving at Crich in December that year.

It was the first tram to be professionally painted at Crich, in 1964, when it acquired a simplified version of the red, teak and white livery that it never carried as a totally enclosed car. The additional lining and embellishments were added over the years but when it came time for a major overhaul in 1977 the opportunity was taken to repaint the car into the green and cream livery in which it arrived. Later, Balcony 40 would receive the red, white and teak livery instead.

GATESHEAD 52

Gateshead No.52 did not acquire this number until its original number '7' was taken up by a batch of new bogie single-deckers including No.5 (page 16) being placed in service in 1927. It formerly operated on the Bensham and Saltwell Park services and came to grief in a serious accident in 1916 when it overturned on Bensham Bank. The car suffered extensive damage to the extent of being written off, and four pedestrians were killed. Somehow, in the course of the next four years it was rebuilt although it is questionable how much of the original remains. Seating was increased from 28 to 32, semi-vestibules were fitted and the truck wheelbase was extended from 6ft to 8ft during 1938, no doubt to handle the increased end weights. Number 52 and sister car 51 operated the Teams route which normally required a single tram, and they did so until it closed in 1951.

One of its motormen, William Southern, purchased No.52 and had it transported to his garden. It was presented to the TMS in 1960 shortly before he died. All these years exposed to the elements did no good at all and, although some minor replacement of rusted panels was done, the car has never run at Crich and is currently stored at Clay Cross awaiting the resources to fund a major restoration.

BLACKPOOL DREADNOUGHT 59

Blackpool, as a rapidly developing seaside resort at the turn of the 19th Century, needed large capacity trams capable of rapid loading and unloading. The 'Dreadnought' class provided both, and they were aptly named because everything about them seemed to be large, be it the extended girder underframing or the over-engineered bogies or indeed the two staircases on each platform depositing alighting passengers right in the path of a following tram. They were either loved or loathed and the latter sentiment centred on the potentially dangerous loading and unloading design.

When Walter Luff arrived on the scene in 1933 as the new General Manager he wasted no time in specifying replacements in the form of open-topped streamliners to complement the Balloon double-deckers and Railcoaches.

BLACKPOOL DREADNOUGHT 59

The days of the Dreadnoughts were numbered but instructions went out that the last, No.59 of 1902, should not be scrapped but set aside for posterity. It languished at Copse Road in the guise of a tool store, gathering dust and losing a few fittings in the process. It re-emerged into daylight to be taken to Rigby Road for restoration as part of the celebrations for the 75th anniversary of the tramway. It re-entered service in 1960 and stayed in Blackpool until 1965 when it came to Crich. It is seen above in 1968, for the Grand Transport Extravaganza, forming a wonderful location for the visiting brass band.

It formed part of the early running fleet until 1970 when body overhaul was needed. It returned to Blackpool, however, for this to be done by the Blackpool Technical College in 1975 and remained in its home town until 1990 when it came back to Crich with a more prominent sag in the underframe betraying that all was not well. It went into storage at Clay Cross where it has remained.

Emotions run high with this particular tram and this is not the place to take sides. Its supporters are anguished that it does not see the light of day or receive attention, being unique and of historical significance to its home town. The counter argument is that as a 'one-off' design it is not really typical and that limited finances dictate that priority should be given to more typical trams that should be restored, particularly when they bring with them a dowry to underwrite the ever increasing costs that the necessary skills can command. Time alone will determine its fate.

JOHANNESBURG 60

When No.60 comes into view, visitors are quite content to assume that it is a typical British open-ended four-wheeled tramcar. Only on close inspection does it become apparent that something is not quite right when reading the notices confirms that they are bilingual. They are in English and Afrikaans. Number 60 was built in Preston, yes, but operated in South Africa. The tram dates from 1906 and originally had saloons with three windows. Rebuilding in 1930 involved re-posting to provide five-window saloons, and parts have been found of even more recent origin. The arrival of new bogie cars in the 'thirties displaced many of the older cars to native routes but No.60 always operated on European routes until it was withdrawn in 1960.

It was the then unavailability of traditional British open ended four-wheelers that prompted the Tramcar Sponsorship Organisation (TSO) to enter into what proved to be protracted negotiations over the purchase and transportation of this convincingly traditional British tram. It eventually arrived at Crich in December 1964. It must also have convinced Granada Television

producers who were looking for a suitable tram to feature in their 1965 production of DH Lawrence's 'Tickets Please'. A Notts & Derby tram was required and Johannesburg 60 was just right for the part. It was dressed accordingly and featured in the play. Unfortunately the very basic electric generation of the day failed just before filming commenced, so, for the camera, it was towed up the line by the diesel loco, propelled down the gradient a short distance and let go!

Its moment in the limelight over, No. 60 retired (or 'rested' as they say in theatrical circles) until the TMS was able to take advantage of job creation programmes in the 1970s designed to relieve unemployment. This allowed a selection of restoration projects to be advanced and the first to benefit was Jo'burg 60, chosen because the car was virtually intact and had a relatively simple livery. It was the success of this project that led directly to other, more ambitious, schemes being brought forward.

Number 60 has continued to benefit from TSO funding, having recently been given new wheelsets allowing it to be returned to service during 2006.

PAISLEY 68

The Paisley District Tramways operated 73 trams. After poor results with the initial fleet, bought on price rather than quality, lessons were obviously learned. As a result, the Company either specified, or was offered, trams based on the London County Council's 'M' class design minus top cover. The builders were Brush and Hurst Nelson (both of whom built for the LCC) and each supplied two batches of five cars. Number 68 was by Hurst Nelson, placed in service in 1919, as a basic open platform, open-top tram. The lower deck is identical to the 'M' class car, essentially a three-window version of the 'E/1' bogie version.

The Paisley Company was taken over in 1923 by neighbouring Glasgow Corporation Tramways. Having newly rid itself of its last open-toppers, there must have been a weary sigh on becoming the proud possessors of another 71! But 68 and its sister cars were far too good to set aside and steps were taken to bring them into line with the contemporary Glasgow Standard cars (like 22, page 25). Within the next ten years all had been modernised as 812 (page 66) taking on the appearance of a tram with a London lower-deck and a Glasgow upper-deck, which is exactly what they were. The class was spread around various depots as equals to the Standards. Number 68 had become 1068 and stabled at Govan Depot, latterly with Yellow Route colour.

Scrapping commenced in 1949. By 1953 only two were left, with 1068 becoming the last, and on the intervention of the Scottish Tramway Museum Society, it was set aside and stored until the Corporation had no room for it. By 1960, when notice to quit arrived, the TMS was beginning to establish facilities at Crich so 1068 arrived in September. It had been given a recently overhauled and re-gauged truck from Standard car 751.

In 1967 work commenced in undoing all the Glasgow features and the car regained its identity as Paisley 68. This was done in several stages and completed under the job creation scheme in 1977. Then the call came for trams to operate at the Glasgow Garden Festival in 1988. Number 68 was offered and accepted. It featured in the Festival's publicity and appeared in posters throughout the London Underground network.

Since its return to Crich the tram has remained within the running fleet and makes an interesting comparison with the two other open-toppers, 45 and 106, and, like them, is a magnet for visitors on sunny days.

In the photograph on the facing page the traditional lining, typical of tramcars throughout the world, can be seen along with the ornate shaded numerals, the name of the undertaking along the quaintly-named 'rocker panels', and a variety of notices giving *'Dos and Don'ts'* to passengers and crews alike.

The municipal coat-of-arms sits proudly in centre stage for all to see.

SHEFFIELD 74

For many years a major gap in the collection was the short canopied top covered tram. Sheffield No.74's resurrection illustrates typical TMS detective work and ingenuity, bearing in mind that there have been no such examples of the type for over 70 years. Originating as a 1900 open top car built by the Electric Railway & Carriage Company in Preston, it acquired a short top cover in 1909 and was sold to the Gateshead & District Tramways in 1922 where open balconies were added. There it remained until the system closed in 1951 and the lower saloon was sold for use as a garden shed.

Trams like 74 continued running in Sheffield until replacement by new cars like 189 (page 52). The top covers from cars 215 and 218 were bought by Tramway Inspector Walter Moorhouse and used to construct a cottage. Sold to the TMS in 1970, 215's top cover was dismantled to provide spares for the other. Then in 1990 74's bottom deck was found near Gateshead, purchased and arrived at Crich that year.

Mainly TSO funded, but also with a Science Museum Grant, the tram was recreated and married to a Peckham Cantilever truck salvaged from Leeds No.110A, held in TMS stock. A fine example of the Crich Workshop creative and recreative skills. Emmet would undoubtedly approve of the appearance!

As constructed this tram was very similar to LCC 106 (page 44), both being built by the Electric Railway & Carriage Company. Number 76 entered service in 1904 and was soon given a domed roof balcony top cover, and by 1923 it had the balconies and platforms enclosed. It was withdrawn in 1947, becoming a cricket pavilion but when tracked down by TMS members it was still at the disused cricket ground near Snaith in Yorkshire, minus truck and controllers. It came to Crich in 1960 and a suitable Brush truck was obtained from Glasgow Corporation's 'School Car', 1017 (ex-Paisley 17) which the Coplawhill Car Works regauged with other cars for Crich before despatch.

Number 76 was undoubtedly the first tram at Crich to undergo ambitious structural alterations and coach-painting to the highest standards. This was done when facilities were just about non-existent. The car was restored to its 1920 condition, and features carved interior woodwork, embossed ceilings and cut glass lamp shades. It operated at the Museum during the period 1973-75 but is currently on display in the Exhibition Hall looking, for all the world, like the manufacturer's 'latest model' in a showroom.

NEWCASTLE 102

Number 102 was built by Hurst Nelson of Motherwell as a Summer Car, a single-decker with open sides, although it would be difficult to tell now unless the cramped platforms with staircases squeezed in are a give-away. Once given upper-decks, many of these 'F' Class cars were upgraded with deeper decency panels, front exits or top covers, but 102 is largely as it was when given a top deck but has air braking. There would be little of the Hurst Nelson construction left after all these subsequent alterations. Despite being somewhat ponderous in its acceleration, with their large carrying capacity these cars could certainly shift the Gosforth Park racing crowds. Their distinctive livery was similar to the earliest style used by Glasgow Corporation.

The cadmium yellow lived on in Newcastle's buses and trolleybuses, and later on the Tyne & Wear Metro stock.

The car was withdrawn in 1949, leaving its home town in April of the following year to be stored locally at Benton and further afield in Bury, Lancashire, on sufferance, as was the case with many of the Society's early acquisitions. When there were still no premises at Crich to provide a permanent home, it was placed on open air display at the Montagu Motor Museum at Beaulieu, Hampshire. Originally flanked by Southampton No.45, it was later joined by a Portsmouth trolleybus as seen here. It spent ten years there before extraction for return to Newcastle for complete reconstruction by local members. Only then did the damage from exposure to the elements become evident, and the car had to be completely re-posted, hence the rebuild thus required took eight years. It eventually came to Crich in 1975 and was placed in the running fleet, nothwithstanding its being a notoriously slow loader (those cramped platforms again).

After the outstanding success of the Glasgow Garden Festival in 1988, those organising the 1990 event in Gateshead decided that there should be a tramway there also. Unfortunately, not having been designed-in from the outset, this feature had to be curtailed to fit the space remaining and the line was shorter but still provided a welcome addition to the attractions. The contribution provided by the TMS for Glasgow was recognised, and approaches were again made, resulting in 102's returning to the North East for the season. It can be seen in service at the Garden Festival on page 91.

LONDON COUNTY COUNCIL 106

This is one of 100 of the original four-wheeled 'B' Class trams intended for lightly trafficked routes. They were built, like Leicester 76 (page 41) by the Electric Railway & Carriage Company in 1903 having the same style of reversed stairs, to which the Metropolitan Police objected – so strongly, that they were soon altered to normal as now displayed. The LCC system was at that time entirely conduit operated. There was no trolley mast, the current being collected by means of a plough carrier between the axles. By 1911 most cars had been given top covers but eight, prior to this, were given trolley masts for operation in Woolwich around 1908-10. This is the form in which 106 has been restored.

The bodywork of the 'B' Class trams was evidently not up to intensive service. During the First World War, many were out of use. Fifty-nine were sold and six loaned to no less than five other operators. Those remaining had been withdrawn by 1925 but 21 were converted as snow brooms by the Kilmarnock Engineering Company (part of English Electric), losing their top decks in the process. This is how No.106 survived as '022' in the Works fleet. It was to have been displayed in the London Transport Museum but was restored by the members of the London County Council Tramways Trust, locally in London, coming to Crich in 1983.

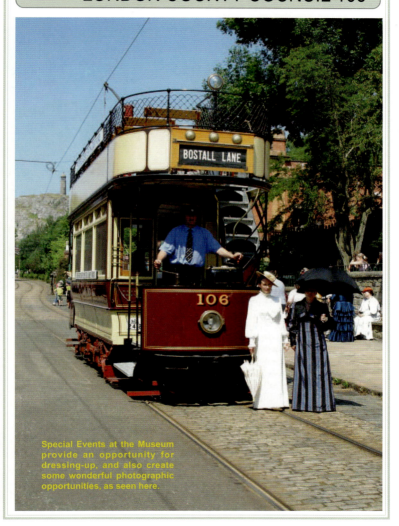

BOSTALL LANE

106

Special Events at the Museum provide an opportunity for dressing-up, and also create some wonderful photographic opportunities, as seen here.

LONDON UNITED 159

This illustration, taken from the Viewing Gallery in the Tramcar Workshop, shows restoration underway on the remains of former London United tramcar No.159 which commenced in 2005, funded by the London County Council Tramways Trust. The car is a 'W' Class example built by GF Milnes of Birkenhead in 1902. These originally had Brill 22E maximum traction bogies and the upper-deck sides featured ornate wrought iron scrollwork. The stairs were of the double-flight 'Robinson' type (named after the LUT General Manager Clifton Robinson). The original 'W' trams were predominantly in a blue route colour livery for the Hampton Court services to Hammersmith and Wimbledon when first placed in service. Fifty of the Class 'W' cars were later given top covers and reclassified 'U' while a further ten were sold to Erith and Walthamstow Corporations. Car 159 was not altered or sold and did not survive to be renumbered into the all-embracing numbering scheme after the formation of London Transport in 1933.

This short-canopied open-top bogie car fills a significant gap in the collection and it will be the only one to recreate the 'Robinson' staircase design. The restoration is expected to take at least a further three years to transform this hulk into a running tram. The recently-opened viewing gallery allows visitors to inspect work in progress.

BLACKPOOL TOASTRACK 166

Seaside towns were the home of toastrack trams, and this fully-open 1927 example comes from Blackpool, a town that went in for them in a big way. It was in use in this guise until the advent of the Second World War, during which it was stored outside while the earlier examples were scrapped. From the mid-1930s they had all carried Walter Luff's green and cream livery.

The newest cars,161-166, were retained for possible departmental use or conversion as illuminated cars. Numbers 165 and 166 took on a new role as BBC mobile outside broadcast cars for televising the resort's famous autumn illuminations, recognising that the best view has always been from a tram! Miniaturisation and changing fashions later rendered them redundant. Number 165 was scrapped in 1968 but 166 remained in Blackpool until 1972 when it was donated to the TMS. Fortunately, there were enough original fitments under its latter-day cladding to provide patterns for a complete restoration that was completed in 1974. Since then 166 has been popular with visitors in good weather. It participated in two contrasting events: driven by the Society's Patron HRH Richard, Duke of Gloucester in 1975, and conveying the coffin of 1981-82 Society President Richard Fairbairn.

BLACKPOOL PANTOGRAPH CAR 167

When Blackpool Corporation took over the Blackpool & Fleetwood Tramroad they found that much of the Company's rolling stock needed replacement. A batch of Pullman trams was purchased from the English Electric Company at Preston in 1928. They featured clerestory roofs which were then enjoying a brief resurgence in fashion. Carrying pantographs in their early years, hence their being known as 'Pantograph Cars', they operated on the service from Fleetwood to Blackpool North Station where thousands of holiday makers entered and left the resort.

Featuring spacious vestibules where luggage could be stacked, and soon being fitted with folding doors to keep out the wind on colder days, the cars were dedicated to this service from 1928 until 1961 when the service passed briefly into the hands of more modern stock.

This example owes its existence, like several in the collection, to having been used as a works car after withdrawal from passenger service. Fortuitously, it retained its original bogies and was truly representative of the original build. It arrived at Crich in 1962, went to Smithills, Bolton, workshop for restoration prior to participating in Blackpool's 1985 Tramways Centenary, then to the Gateshead Garden Festival in 1990 and back to Blackpool again for the Blackpool & Fleetwood Tramroad's own Centenary in 1998.

LEEDS 180

'Bob' Horsfield, General Manager of the Leeds Corporation Tramways, died in office in 1931 when nearly half of the 104 cars that bore his name were in service. He had designed these new four-wheeled cars, though they were also known as 'Showboats' after the popular Jerome Kern musical of the day. These were well-proportioned, sturdy and versatile cars that could be used anywhere on the Leeds system. They represent what is probably the zenith of traditional British tramcar design before the advent of domed roofs and streamlining. The production batch was built by the Brush Electrical Engineering Company of Loughborough, and many lasted until final closure of the Leeds system in November 1959.

Number 180 was one that did, and ran in the closing procession, by that time renumbered '189', which it carried when it arrived at Crich. Since Crich already had a Sheffield tram of that number, it seemed appropriate to renumber the Leeds car back to 180. A later acquisition, overleaf, upset the logic.

Horsfield 180 has been restored in the striking maroon and cream livery latterly carried, enhanced with restrained lining-out that was omitted by Leeds in the final years. Previously it had been painted in various versions of blue, and was in khaki during the war.

PRAGUE 180

Many of the trams at Crich have had chequered histories but none more so than this one. It operated in Czechoslovakia until 1967 when it was offered to The Tramway Museum Society by the tramcar manufacturing industry in eastern Europe. It represented a type of car which would enhance the collection, and the generous offer was readily and happily accepted.

Unfortunately, international affairs stepped in, and the Russian occupation of Czechoslavakia took place, in 1968, just as 180 crossed the border out of its home country. All communication with the outside world was cut and the party accompanying the tram were unable to make contact with their relatives and friends back home to make sure they were safe. After some nail-biting days they were eventually able to re-establish contact and then to return home. Before they did so, however, they arrived at Crich right in the middle of the first Grand Transport Extravaganza. With great flourish, 180 was taken off its trailer straight on to the Crich track and driven smartly up the line.

Whilst all the Museum's exhibits are 'special', this one is perhaps rather more so, and it will usually be found safe and sound in the Exhibition Hall where visitors not in the know will ponder over the unfamiliar signwriting on its cream rocker panels and elsewhere. The livery of bright red and cream is often seen on trams operating in the city of Prague whenever that city is in the news and television crews film in that capital's streets.

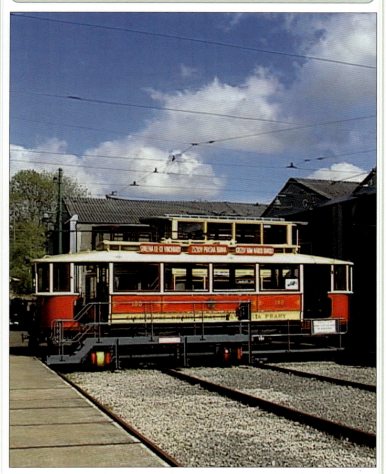

Prague 180 seen standing on the traverser. This is used to move trams from one depot to another, or from one road to another, or into and out of the Exhibition Hall.

SHEFFIELD 189

This well maintained system was able progressively to keep its fleet up to date by replacing outmoded cars with new ones, rather than by modernising existing stock. Hence cars like No.74 (page 40) were being replaced from the late 1920s by new Standard cars such as No.189. Most were built in the Corporation's workshops between 1928 and 1936. The earlier cars featured the traditional Prussian blue and cream livery with gold lining-out. Sheffield would not consider bogie cars on their steep gradients and these cars were capacious – Glasgow would probably have mounted them on bogies. The wheels were of large diameter at 33in and the 50hp motors were made locally by Metropolitan-Vickers. Number 189 was placed in service in 1934, mainly running on the Ecclesall–Middlewood and Fulwood–Malin Bridge routes, being allocated to Holme Lane Depot before transfer to Tenter Street.

Sheffield 189 was another tram not intended for preservation. Car 195 was the first choice, but was found to be in inferior condition. The Corporation donated 189 to the TMS and, after a special tour in March 1958, the car was withdrawn and stored, re-emerging in the final closing procession. The need to find a home for 189 led directly to the discovery of Crich – the rest is history.

SHEFFIELD 264

The later production of Sheffield's '1927 Standard' trams carried a more modern livery that was a foretaste of things to come. This took the form of an improved version, first appearing in 1935. These trams had domed roofs and raked upper deck pillars. The traditional quarter-light lower deck windows were also superseded by panelling and extractor ventilators, with the destination indicator centrally positioned. Although to the same basic dimensions as their predecessors, the new domed roof cars were most attractive vehicles, carrying the modern azure blue and cream livery extremely well. Sixty-seven were placed in service before wartime restrictions came and effectively stopped production, but later a further 14 utility versions were built during the war as replacements for bomb-damaged cars.

Number 264 dates from 1937, operating from Crookes to Woodseats and, later, Handsworth. The selection of the other Sheffield trams (other than 74) was made in advance, but 264 was rescued after the closure, having been still working in normal service until the final day, arriving at Crich in December 1960. It has been repainted twice. The full pre-war livery was re-applied in 1968-69, as shown above, but it has since acquired the later variation.

Like 189, the car embodies light-construction bodywork and there is evident working of the joints when running. Both cars await full workshop attention.

This location has been transformed by the growth of a splendid line of trees, sett-paved roadway and York-stone pavement, as visitors can see.

OPORTO 273

The Society had been seeking to acquire an Oporto semi-convertible car for many years before No. 273 eventually arrived in June 1996, in a dowdy blue and white all-over advertising livery. It carries bodywork in which the window sashes are designed to lift upwards into the car body – ideal for warmer climates. Its dilapidated state was soon transformed by the Crich workshop.

The reversed maximum traction bogies were stripped and rebuilt, and the bodywork taken apart and re-assembled with new timbers as needed. Of note are the rattan cane seats – precursors of fabric covered sprung upholstery. The car was repainted in the post-war Oporto mustard and cream livery which their No.9 (page 20) carried when it first came to Crich. The restoration work was completed by 2002 when the car re-entered service receiving an award from the Heritage Railway Association.

Another reason why this car was sought is that it fills the gap in the history of the development of the American streetcar. Whilst 273 is the oldest, New York 674 represents the pre-PCC era and The Hague's 1147 is a PCC car. Purchase of these cars avoided the huge costs of Transatlantic shipping.

In 1936, Blackpool Corporation already had its fleet of modern Railcoaches, streamlined Balloon and open-top cars in service, yet was still obliged to resort to hiring trams from the adjacent Lytham St Anne's fleet at peak periods. It was the closure of the latter system that prompted the need to order a further 20 single-deckers.

This time, the successful tenderer was Brush, and, to avoid infringing patents, there were subtle differences in the design that set their model apart from their earlier English Electric counterparts. Many consider the Brush cars could be regarded as the zenith of Blackpool's pre-war designs in terms of appearance and luxury. Although reduced in numbers, many still operate, but they have been substantially altered over the intervening years.

Number 298 (latterly numbered 635) had been less altered than sister cars and it was decided to withdraw the car rather than carry out major rebuilding work. It was rescued and has been partially restored over a period exceeding 20 years, off-site in various locations, but latterly at the Mode Wheel, Salford, workshops. A great deal of work has been done to restore lost features as will be seen, but the car has finally come to Crich to have the job completed and take advantage of the equipment and skills available.

SUNDERLAND 100

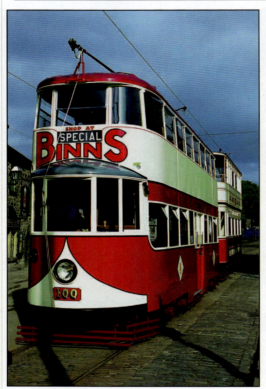

This is another 'one-off' at Crich, but, like LCC No.1 (page 12), is highly significant for the future designs it spawned. It was the last of five experimental trams that led to the design of the Underground Group's 'Feltham' trams and thus represented a truly 'giant step for tramkind' when compared with their contemporaries.

The car was placed in service by the Metropolitan Electric Tramways as No. 331 in December 1930; its appearance was an improvement on the 100 production cars in being symmetrical around the central entrance. Its unique livery included crimson on the upper side panels, displacing the normal cream.

It operated on the North London Whetstone-Cricklewood service but the advancing replacement trolleybuses caused its withdrawal. The production cars migrated to South London, but No. 331 had to be withdrawn in August 1936 as the central entrance-well prevented the fitting of plough gear. The Sunderland Corporation Transport Manager had an eye for bargains and acquired the car. It ran there until 1952, numbered 100, as seen above.

Importantly, the Registered Design and associated patents had been sold to English Electric, leading to their later examples of centre-entrance trams that operated in Blackpool, Sunderland, Darwen and Aberdeen.

METROPOLITAN 331

The late JW Fowler, founder of the Light Railway Transport League, acquired the car and it was given temporary storage in various garages and depots. It eventually arrived at Crich looking very sad, and, in the early days, had a file all to itself labelled 'too hard', for its restoration would be the most daunting ever. This needed a catalyst that came in the form of the Gateshead Garden Festival in 1990, where there was a need for local cars. This provided the spur to restore the car as Sunderland No.100 and it was formally handed over to officials in that form. Garden Festivals relied heavily on sponsorship and British Steel offered to sponsor this 'steel' car. They required its repainting in their blue and white corporate livery. A little more confidence from the Festival Company officials could have avoided this. They could have offered the upper side panels but no, they agreed to the transformation and lost the local identity. Perhaps they felt that a refusal would have lost a valued sponsor. (However, a similar request to have Edinburgh 35 painted in the British Gas livery was politely refused in 1988 and there was no rancour).

When 'British Steel No.100' returned after a successful stay in Gateshead, where it carried HRH The Princess Royal, the opportunity was taken to repaint the tram in its London MET livery, once more numbered 331, as seen.

LEEDS 345

Number 345 entered service in 1921 as a traditional open-balcony tram, one of 30 placed in service after the First World War. To augment the fleet of more recent trams, all but one of these, and five earlier cars, were duly modernised with enclosed balconies and platform doors during the period 1935-42, bringing them up to the standard of Horsfield Car No.180 (page 49). They were not, of course, new trams but still of pleasing appearance.

The upper-deck bulkheads were removed and the end panels upswept to incorporate built-in route number and destination indicators, freeing up the front window of the upper-deck for forward vision denied on the earlier enclosed cars. Leeds 345 was one of the last 'Converts' (as they were known) being upgraded in 1939. Most were withdrawn during 1949 but No. 345 was taken to the Kirkstall Road Works for overhaul in 1948. However, it was officially withdrawn two months after its arrival there. It is thought that the bodywork was found to be defective. It survived, however, by being converted into a static Joiners' Shop at the Works and then in Swinegate depot. The Leeds Transport Historical Society (LTHS) bought it in 1959 for preservation and that is how it came to be at Crich in December of that year.

It looked a sorry sight with its faded 1945 blue paint, by then completely matt, and with bulging lower-deck sides and distorted pillars. Many fittings and seating had been removed. For a few years, valiant attempts were maintained to keep the weather and further deterioration at bay. However, as the general appearance of other cars improved, some of the less glamorous exhibits were consigned to off-site storage, leaving behind trams that were either restored already or were easier to tackle. Gone, perhaps, but not forgotten.

The funding of what, by any standards, was a complete rebuild, was taken over by the Tramcar Sponsorship Organisation, augmenting the efforts of the LTHS. Number 345 was brought back and went through the process of being taken apart, re-assembled with new or restored parts and equipment, eventually being completed in 2006. A splendid launch was arranged in true TMS fashion and this 'Princess' of trams, appropriately in 'Princess Blue' livery, was accepted into the running fleet on Saturday 1st April, forty-seven years after arriving at the Crich Museum.

It is seen above gleaming in the evening sunshine, in all its newly-found glory, to greet Keith Terry, the incoming Society President for the year 2006/7.

LEEDS 399

Number 399 was the second tram to arrive at Crich, having left its home city before the closure of the tramway system. It was not until the end of 1990 that its long process of restoration was complete; the pace of this process speeding up considerably once the car was called into the Workshops. It originally entered service in 1925, not very different from No. 345 of four years earlier. It did, however, have the balconies enclosed as built and although carrying the primrose and chocolate livery, it was the last tram to enter service in this style. It represented the end of an era in another respect for long-serving General Manager JB Hamilton's successor had taken over before 399 was completed.

The blue livery was applied in 1930 and a bow collector fitted in 1937. With air braking, it was used on the hilly services, such as to Beeston, hence the unofficial title 'Beeston Air Brake' car. Number 399 finished its service career in 1951 but was subsequently used as depot shunter at Kirkstall Road Works, and latterly Swinegate. In performing these duties, many parts were removed, including the compressor, a set of track brakes, some seats and much of the glazing. This all had to be sourced or manufactured for another superb restoration, and one of the most attractive liveries in the collection?

SHEFFIELD 510

Sheffield's first generation trams finished on a high note, principally the closing procession on 8th October 1960. It so impressed guests from Glasgow Corporation that they resolved to do the same when their turn came in 1962. The highlight of the Sheffield procession was tram No.510, magnificently outshopped with historical highlights of the Sheffield tramway history hand-painted on the upper-side panels. The car had enjoyed a brief service life, having been built in 1950, one of a batch of 35 cars. Sheffield built nearly all of its own trams, but this post-war order went to Charles Roberts of Wakefield. They are better known for railway wagon manufacture, but were seeking bus and tram orders at the time. The 'Roberts Cars' were of robust construction and were to prove troublesome to the scrap merchants in later years. Fortunately, two survive and the collection at Crich has number 510 suitably lettered 'Sheffield's Last Tram'.

No doubt many would have believed that on the occasion of its first repaint, 510 would revert to normal livery, as the hand-painted panels would be impossible to replicate. Fortunately, the doubters were proved wrong, and they are still extant on replacement panels for all to admire in this, the ultimate development of the traditional British four-wheeled double-deck tramcar.

LEEDS 600

Number 600 has had a chequered career and has its origins as the first Sunderland Corporation tram to carry the number '85'. Built by the Brush Company in 1931 it was intended for the Villette Road route. Its length exceeded 41ft and, being a 'one-off', it was placed in storage at the beginning of the Second World War. Leeds was toying with the idea of tram subways and bought the tram in 1944. It would have become the prototype subway car and made several night-time excursions bearing the number '288'.

It was as long ago as 1949 when conversion to its present state actually started and it was to take nearly five years to complete the transformation. Leeds acquired parts for it from other systems including Southampton, Manchester, Glasgow, London Transport and Liverpool, the latter being the source of the EMB bogies. The finished result was a centre entrance car with tapered ends to achieve clearances on curves. It was renumbered 600 and operated briefly on the Hunslet route until premature withdrawal in 1957.

It was donated to the TMS by a pioneer member but, although it has been repainted and retains a cared-for appearance, the bogies are fragile with developing fractures and the decision was taken to remove the tram to the off-site store at Clay Cross to which it was despatched in December 2005.

   While the reconstruction of Leeds No. 600 was under way, the Transport Department placed orders with local bus builders Charles H Roe for two brand new centre-entrance single-deckers to be numbered 601 and 602. These would represent the ultimate first generation British trams, particularly No.602 which was the more sophisticated of the two. This car was all-electric and featured VAMBAC (Variable Automatic Multinotch Braking & Acceleration Control). This was a complex mechanical device whose function in today's modern trams would be carried out using solid state control.

   In 1953 this was as far as tramway technology had gone. It was similar to equipment then in use in Blackpool and on one tram in Glasgow (their 1005), but both undertakings had experienced some difficulties with it. The way of the pioneer is not always straightforward.

   Entering service around the time of the Coronation of Queen Elizabeth, the two new cars were outshopped in a royal purple livery, eventually settling down to operating the unobtrusive Hunslet route. The significance of 602 was appreciated and the car came to Crich in 1960. It has been overhauled several times since then and is still a vision in its striking livery.

NEW YORK 3rd AVENUE 674

This is the only genuine American car at Crich, although there are others that illustrate their development. Yet No. 674 did not come directly from the USA. Built in 1939 by the Third Avenue Transit Company, No. 674 was one of their 'Z' class, designed for one man operation and seating 46 passengers within its wide saloon. With World War II over, European capitals were on their knees to the point of exhaustion and as part of the American Marshall Aid programme, No. 674 and a further 41 such cars, were exported to Vienna. Number 674 became Wiener Verkehrsbetriebe No.4225 and ran there until withdrawal in 1969 when the British Ambassador to Austria formally received the tram before it set off for Crich, arriving in April 1970. It operated for six years as 4225 with its pantograph mounted on a raised extension to reach the UK height overhead wires designed for double-decker tramcars.

The New York livery was restored in 1979 and twin trolley poles were fitted. Most recently 674 has been part of a static display explaining the story of the President's Conference Committee (PCC) cars.

It is not generally known that No.674 was seriously considered as a static exhibit for the 1988 Glasgow Garden Festival. It would have been a major sponsor's hospitality venue where its wide saloon would have been put to good use.

It is seen here against the backdrop of the old workshop building wall, before the new splendid brick facade was constructed.

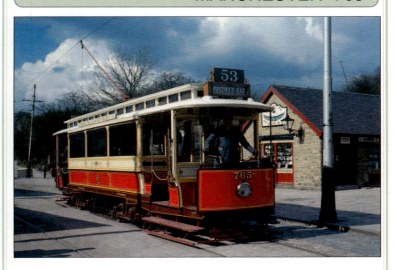

Manchester is generally perceived as the home of the very traditional large tramcar, with maximum traction bogies, yet there was one route (the '53') that had to rely on single-deckers to negotiate low railway bridges that prevented double-decker operation. Combination, or 'California', cars were operated, and each comprised an enclosed centre-saloon with open accommodation at each end. The total seating complement was for 40 passengers. Number 765 was one of these, and was placed in service in 1914 to an already dated design. When new General Manager R Stuart Pilcher came from Edinburgh in 1929, where he had left their tramways in excellent fettle, he wasted no time in seeking to withdraw the route 53 trams, duly replacing them with lowbridge buses in 1930.

Number 765 ended up on a farm near Huddersfield, until 1960 when it was rescued by a group of Manchester members and brought to Crich. With virtually no workshop facilities and no available covered accommodation, they fought a losing battle with the elements until eventually the car returned to Manchester for the restoration work to begin in earnest. The bogies came from the Hill of Howth Tramway, re-gauged to the British standard. It operated at Crich in 1977-78 but its normal home is at Heaton Park in Manchester, although it was another participant at the Blackpool Centenary in 1985.

GLASGOW 812

Number 812 is a direct product of an 1896 whistle-stop tour of the Eastern Seaboard of the United States by Glasgow Corporation's Tramways Rolling Stock Engineer and General Manager. Despite seasickness they picked up many ideas. Not least was the distinctive cadmium orange livery. After a false start with single-deckers, Glasgow's Standard tram emerged in 1898 and there would eventually be over a thousand. All had been modernised by 1935 and many gave 50 year's service – 812 gave 60, although this nearly did not happen. But for the Second World War, 812 would have been given a new body to make better use of its modern running gear. Had it not been for the Suez Crisis of 1956-57 the car would have been scrapped, instead it received a further overhaul. Finally, but for the TMS, it would have been scrapped in 1960. Instead it came to Crich.

Glasgow 812 has been restored in its 1930s condition and chosen to portray the Yellow Route livery. As one of the earliest Standards, it went through the processes of acquiring a top cover with open ends, then vestibuled platforms and finally the tram was totally enclosed. The original bodywork was never designed with these additions in mind, or the high service speeds and rapid braking latterly achieved. Number 812 celebrated its centenary on 6th August 2000 (two days after The Queen Mother's) and, accordingly, this was appropriately celebrated at Crich.

LIVERPOOL 869

This is one of three cars whose origins and development can be traced back to LCC No.1 (page 12). Number 869 also represents the outcome of production line manufacture in Liverpool's Edge Lane Works during 1936-37 that took advantage of prefabrication techniques. The pinnacle of their efforts was this, the 'Liner' class. There were 163 and they helped buck the trend

of tramway decline. They underwent privations during the Second World War and evident total neglect afterwards. Too late for some, a programme of renovation was put in hand from the early 1950s but, despite re-inforcement strapping, their lightweight bodywork did not have lasting qualities.

By then, tramway abandonment was well under way and Glasgow Corporation accepted an offer to purchase 46 of the (alleged) best trams. This prolonged their use until 1960, by which time Glasgow had run out of patience with them. This ensured that a rather battered 1055, alias Liverpool 869, was preserved and despite its condition, it was magnificently restored in Liverpool and Crich to confirm just how splendid the Liverpool 'Liner' really was in its heyday. Now in the running fleet it has totally rebuilt bogies.

HALLE 902

Such has been the success of the Access Tram (Berlin 3006 – pages 75/6), with its wheelchair lift, that it was necessary to have back up. Another East German tram was acquired for this purpose in the form of Halle 902, arriving in 2005. This is a product of the CKD Tatra Company in Prague, capable of turning out over 1,000 trams every year, and is one of only two Tatra-PCCs with driving cabins at each end. It also incorporates a development of the PCC-type equipment to be found in Leeds No. 602 (page 63).

The car has four motors and a prodigious appetite for current – such that it can consume a very large part of the total sub-station output, a matter which is having to be addressed. It incorporates an odd mixture of highly sophisticated and primitive electrical equipment, making it of great interest to students of tramcar technology.

The red and cream livery is typical of former Eastern Bloc tramways and will be familiar to those who have enjoyed holidays in Eastern Europe and beyond. An earlier style can also be found on Prague Number 180 (pages 50/1).

GLASGOW 1100

For much of its life Glasgow number 1100 seems to have been a test bed for experiments. One of 30 Hurst Nelson maximum-traction bogie cars built in 1928-29, 1100 was soon called to the Car Works to have Brill bogies replace the Kilmarnock Engineering versions that were prone to derailing. It was back in the Works to have Kilmarnock Bogies reinstated at the start of the Second World War when the bodywork was transformed by the forming of tapered curved ends. At first they incorporated reversed stairs, and then field control was installed, to be replaced with contactor control. A pantograph was fitted for a while. It was the only tram with route colour indicators using illuminated coloured lenses, although these had been taken from a Standard car where they had been originally fitted.

Bristling with all those unique features 1100 did not see much city use and was usually confined to shipyard extra duties to and from Clydebank. Scheduled for scrapping as early as 1949 the car survived until the end of the Glasgow system in 1962, being a regular performer on enthusiasts' tours of the system, and was the last to leave the Car Works before arriving at Crich where it operated in 1965-76.

Currently No.1100 is at Clay Cross in storage. Why was 1100 selected for all the experiments when others in the class were not? Probably because its number was easy to remember for some Transport Department clerk!

Outside builders were commissioned by Glasgow Corporation to build a fleet of 50 'Standard Double Bogie' cars to compete head on with independent buses. Number 1115 was one of the last of these, built by Hurst Nelson and entering service in 1929. It has been described at Crich as a 'refined 812' which it is, sharing electrical and mechanical equipment and many bodywork parts. Much of the refinement lies in the very resilient Kilmarnock Engineering Co. bogies that provide a very smooth ride, but they did not take kindly to right angled junctions in the city centre. Derailments were common and this caused their transfer to the straight

east-west services that became their domain. This required them to be repainted with Red Route colours, replacing the former Green.

They remained on them until the last was withdrawn in 1961, and 1115 came to Crich in 1962. Since running between 1971 and 1976, 1115 has not been in the operational fleet. It nearly went to the 1988 Glasgow Garden Festival and was repainted, just in case. Most recently it has formed the centrepiece of the 'Trams in the Dark' display. When will it see the light of day again?

THE HAGUE 1147

The Hague's post-war replacement tram fleet adopted the American PCC (President's Conference Committee) design even to the specification of the bodywork which, on the first examples, incorporated standee windows. The later versions, represented by 1147, had larger and more conventional windows with a more satisfactory appearance, to European eyes at least. It was built under licence by La Brugeoise, Belgium, in 1957, incorporating electrical equipment by ACEC (Ateliers des Constructions Electriques de Charleroi). It survived to be one of the 23 PCC cars remaining in service on 30th June, 1993, their last day of operation in passenger service. It spent some time in the open at Zichtenburg Depot before being placed under cover there in November of that year, awaiting its journey to Crich. Number 1147 was eventually shipped by North Sea Ferries in January 1994, arriving via the port of Hull.

Since then, the car has been restored, with its original cream and green livery, but, being single-ended, there are limitations to operational use and so it forms part of the PCC exhibition, where it makes an interesting comparison with New York 3rd Avenue Transit No. 674. The latter, having been built in 1939, actually post-dated many PCC trams in America.

GLASGOW 1282

Glasgow Corporation Transport modernised its entire fleet of Standard trams by 1935. It was realised even then that new bodies would be required to make better use of their new equipment. Yet there was an urgent need for additions to the fleet and, with the Empire Exhibition to be held in the city in 1938, they commissioned a new fleet of bogie double-deckers, initially to operate the Exhibition, with 1282 being one of the last. Their design can be traced back to LCC No.1 but construction incorporated lessons learned since then.

Principally, the bodies were neither too heavy nor too light, and the Coplawhill Car Works avoided the use of curved glass and panel beating where this might be vulnerable to damage. They were spacious and opulently finished trams so as to impress visitors to Glasgow attending the Exhibition.

They were described as being amongst the finest trams in Europe at the time they were introduced, a soubriquet few would challenge when looking at the detailed finish and experiencing the smooth and powerful ride.

Number 1282 operated from various depots, but is associated with the Paisley services. It was selected to run in the Glasgow closing procession, for which it was smartened up, and then, most importantly, to run as Clydebank's last tram two days afterwards in September 1962. It thus became the last of the first generation trams in Scotland to operate on the

public highway. The car was purchased by the then Scottish Tramway Museum Society and arrived at Crich in 1963. It has been rebuilt and operated regularly but currently awaits rectification of the effects of corrosion in the underframing. It is seen left, in service, and above with No. 1100 for comparison, on display in the Exhibition Hall.

GLASGOW 1297

Any lingering thoughts about making better use of the modern equipment with which elderly Glasgow Standard trams had been running were dispelled after World War II. The trams had coped well, but that same equipment was then six years older and new trams were needed. The first emerged in 1948, officially 'Coronation Mark II' class but generally known as 'Cunarders'. They were intended to be an improvement on the pre-war (by then Mark I) Coronations, but lost many of the expensive, or maintenance-intensive, features like ventilation fans and sealed windows. Bodywork was smoothed off and the bogies were supplied by Maley & Taunton with inside frames that created some initial instability problems. Electrical equipment was very similar to that in the pre-war Coronations. There were 100 Cunarders and initially all went to Newlands depot, with 1297 entering service at the very end of 1948.

Two have survived, including the last to be built, but it is 1297 that has had the higher profile. It went to Blackpool for the 1985 Centenary Celebrations there, creating a favourable impression with its lively performance. Then it went back to Glasgow as one of five trams operating at the Garden Festival three years later. It saw no service at Crich for many years but has recently taken No.1282's place, often being used by Ultimate Driving Experience hopefuls, seen to be a 'forgiving car'.

LONDON TRANSPORT 1622

Number 1622 represents the LCC 'E/1' class – the largest class of trams in the UK at well over 1,000. They had been modernised by the LCC in the 1920s and were inherited by London Transport on its formation in 1933. Trolleybuses were to replace the trams, but this would take time and selected members of the class were 'rehabilitated' to give further service until the conversion programme was completed. This was interrupted by World War II and buses would take over from the trams after that. Although E/1s continued in service in both rehabilitated and unmodified condition until 1951, No.1622 was one of a small number sold after the war as holiday homes, hence its escape from the scrapyard.

   The car was found by the London County Council Tramways Trust (LCCT) and given a most thorough rebuild, part of which involved being given a new upper-deck constructed to the original drawings by the Museum's workshop. Bogies were available from a Feltham tram that had been destroyed, and this dictated that a rehabilitated E/1 would be the outcome of the restoration, as running for London Transport in the 1930s. The work was completed in 1999 and No.1622 has been in the running fleet since. Although withdrawal of the last (first generation) London tram took place seven years before Crich was available, no less than nine have been retrieved or restored.

BERLIN 3006 – THE ACCESS TRAM

BERLIN 3006 – THE ACCESS TRAM

The Disability Discrimination Act (DDA) strikes fear in many who have to implement its requirements, and there is much ignorance as to what is needed in its loose wording. The National Tramway Museum has recognised its obligations and also that its vehicles, with high steps and narrow entrance-ways were not built with access for wheelchairs or the infirm in mind. Their solution has been to provide an 'Access Tram', and this is in the form of a Berlin BVG-type TZ69 2-axle double-ended car, number 3006, built in 1969.

Number 3006 is of 'solid' construction not untypical of the former eastern block, with features that are earlier than its years would suggest. The sliding door mechanism sounds as if it could drive the Cleveland Transporter Bridge, but the tram has its own charm. It has been fitted with a wheelchair lift and space provided for securing wheelchairs inside. This facility has been much appreciated by those who have used it and, such has been the demand, that the second Access Tram was acquired in the form of Halle No. 902 as back up. By coincidence, this has also come from the former Eastern Germany and is described on page 68.

STEAM TRAM – Number 47 *aka* John Bull

Steam trams, where operated, were generally used between the horse and electric traction periods, and enabled heavy loads to be hauled that would have taxed horses. Number 47 is a Wilkinson vertical boilered version built by Beyer, Peacock in 1885. It was exported to Sydney, Australia, as a demonstrator, and nick-named *John Bull* whilst there. It failed to make an impression due to its heavy fuel consumption and indifferent steaming. Beyer, Peacock took it back and by 1890 it was performing shunting duties at their works having been numbered '2'. For this purpose the wheel valances, necessary for street running, were taken off and railway-type buffers added. As a tramway locomotive it had double-ended controls but these were modified for single-end working. A new boiler was installed in 1930 and a new exhaust superheater in 1958 before withdrawal the following year. It was discovered by the TMS, and Beyer, Peacock kindly re-profiled the wheels to operate on grooved tramway rail before making the locomotive available for use at Crich.

Number 47 was in steam by 1966, four years after arriving. Initially it ran minus the buffers and still minus the valances. Over the years it regained all the tramway features and was repainted in a chocolate lined-out style. Its dedicated restorers had their triumph in the course of the 1985 Blackpool Centenary cavalcade and, by good fortune, this coincided with the tram's own Centenary.

HORSE DRAWN TOWER WAGON

Many tramway systems used converted trams, or purpose-built tower wagons, for overhead line inspection. This was especially true where access to the overhead was required on reserved tracks that did not have paved road surfaces. Blackpool No. 4 was fitted with an overhead inspection tower for a while before retirement and Leeds No. 2 is a purpose-built example. Before (and after) petrol or diesel lorry chassis were available or reliable, horse-drawn tower wagons were common, and the example at Crich came from the Manchester Corporation Tramways. Sufficient municipal pride was invested in it that it carries a lined-out version of the tramway livery, with the tower painted yellow to make it conspicuous to other road users.

RAIL MOUNTED TOWER WAGON – TW3

Like all proper tramways, the Crich operation has its own works car fleet, and like any other tramway, the overhead wires require to be inspected and maintained not only because most of the fittings are not new, having been salvaged from withdrawn tramway and trolleybus systems, but because they have been installed to handle mixed current collection operation (trolley poles, bow collectors and pantographs) with the additional wear-and-tear that this implies at junctions.

The track is not all sett-paved, and there is consequently a need for a rail-mounted overhead inspection tower wagon which is not an exhibit but a normal workhorse, seen here providing a safe platform for repairs to the overhead at the depot approach.

BLACKPOOL STEEPLE CAB LOCO

This is a typical steeple cab locomotive built in 1927, originally used to haul coal wagons from the LMS sidings at Fleetwood to the Thornton Gate Coal Depot. A similar example ran in Glasgow from the Fairfield Shipyard, and they shared one thing in common. Both operated along the tram tracks, thus meriting a place in the Crich Collection. The coal traffic, for which the Blackpool locomotive needed all of its 2 x 57hp motor output, ceased in 1949 and it was eventually withdrawn in 1965 after very intermittent use.

The TMS could see several uses for it, and purchased it. On arrival at Crich the buffers were immediately removed to avoid damage to other trams being shunted. It was repainted in the red and white lined-out livery of General Manager Charles Furness' era, but has since reverted to the latter-day two shades of green version, forming a useful constituent of the Works Fleet.

It is seen above in the depot entrance, with a display of tramway notices and stop signs forming the backdrop.

LEEDS TOWER WAGON

Leeds Tower Car 2 has its origins in 1925 when a tower-assembly salvaged from a former horse-drawn wagon was mounted onto a petrol railcar chassis. This then allowed access to the tower-car before the overhead was erected or energised on new lengths of reserved track. In 1931 the body structure was mounted on the truck taken from withdrawn electric tram No.110A.

Leeds changed over from trolleys to bow collectors progressively through the later 1930s, and No.2 ran for a while with one bow collector and one trolley pole and has been restored to illustrate this. When sister car No.1 was scrapped, No. 2 took its number and its Peckham Cantilever truck, and in this form survived to the end of the Leeds system in November 1959.

The car was set aside for the Middleton Railway Preservation Society but after sustaining some damage at the hands of vandals, the Leeds Tramway Historical Society took it over and restored it before arrival at Crich.

CARDIFF WATER CAR 131

This is the only representative at Crich from the Principality of Wales, and is another unlikely survivor. It is not a converted passenger car, but one built for the purpose of watering tracks and in so doing also laying the dust on the road surfaces. The tank is concealed by panelling. Number 131 was built by Brush in 1905, originally with a Brill truck, but this was changed by 1920 for what is thought to be a Hurst Nelson version and this truck was modified to carry out rail-scrubbing duties. It survived right up to, and beyond, the end of the Cardiff Tramways, being the last survivor, and was presented to the Museum Committee of the Light Railway Transport League from which emerged the TMS. It was given a light restoration in Cardiff and stored there before becoming the first tram to arrive at Crich in 1959. At first it resided at the entrance, normally covered in tarpaulins.

With fifty years of the Tramway Museum at Crich approaching in 2009 there are movements afoot to enable this distinctive and significant little car to be returned from Clay Cross, where it now resides, for restoration to celebrate the arrival of the first tram and the new era in tramway preservation. It would be a worthy achievement.

SHEFFIELD RAIL GRINDER CAR 330

Sheffield was short of trams during World War II, and examined options for acquiring second-hand cars to maintain adequate services. After discarding offers of surplus London trams, the Transport Department settled on the purchase of trams from Newcastle and Bradford. Ten came from Bradford, including 330. They acquired the totally-enclosed balconies denied to Bradford's four-wheelers by its 4ft 0in gauge through concerns over wind resistance, having been re-gauged by Sheffield to standard, thus obviating the original problem.

The arrival of the new Sheffield Roberts cars allowed the second hand acquisitions to be withdrawn, but 330 – originally Bradford 251 – was set aside in 1951 for conversion to a water car. The top deck was taken off and a steel-framed trolley gantry installed. The platform vestibules were enhanced, and the entrances narrowed to reduce draughts, whilst luxury coach-type trafficators were fitted into the dash plates.

Number 330 was repainted into full passenger fleet livery, and survived to the end of the first generation Sheffield Tramways in 1960. It was rescued from Thomas Ward's scrapyard and came to Crich in December of that year. It was soon subjected to extensive overhaul and has formed a useful member of the works fleet ever since, as well as being an attractive exhibit demonstrating the rolling stock engineer's ingenuity.

OTHER WORKS VEHICLES

Time was when all movements of rolling stock at Crich were undertaken by crow-bars, point irons and human effort. The arrival of diesel shunters changed all that, and there are two. The first arrived in 1963 and not too much is known about its origins. It has always been known at the Museum as 'Rupert', the nick-name of the Museum's volunteer who engineered the regauging from 600mm to standard-gauge. It has been in continuous service ever since, apart from overhauls, and is possibly the smallest standard gauged diesel locomotive still in use.

The sister shunter is 'GMJ', originally used at Crich in quarry days, and seen above. It was rescued by the TMS in 1965 from is latter-day home in a shed at Ambergate where it had been damaged by fire. This was found not to have caused as much damage as had been feared, and the locomotive was thoroughly overhauled, re-gauged with axles machined from BR DMUs, and supported by side frame extensions. The work was completed successfully by December 1969 and 'GMJ' has been in regular service since.

OTHER WORKS VEHICLES

Glasgow Corporation Tramways had a large fleet of works cars even to the extent of having one specially built for cable laying. "No.1" from their Mains Department was rescued and came to Crich. It was complete with its own trailer and, although No.1 itself resides at Clay Cross, the trailer has been adapted from its original use in hauling cable drums to act as a mobile welding truck, as shown in the accompanying illustration.

There are two other trailers comprising a Leeds flat truck with removable sides and used for conveying permanent way materials, and a 1 ton hand operated rail crane that came from the permanent way yard in Sheffield.

Despite a vague resemblance to children's buggies found in large supermarkets, this battery electric tug was formerly used by the Royal Mail to haul trains of railway station mail trolleys between sorting offices and station platforms. It was built by Electricars of Atherstone in 1993 and was

purchased by the Museum five years later when it became redundant. It is now used to tow electric tramcars within the depot and workshop area during repair and maintenance. Its diminutive size may conceal the fact that it can tow the heaviest trams in the fleet and has been called upon to recover a failed tram from the Townend terminus back to the workshop. It is the postal origins that cause it to be known universally as "Postman Pat" rather than by its cumbersome Royal Mail fleet number 2380060.

BRUSSELS SNOW BROOM 96

Not all tram systems had snow brooms. As seen on page 44, London had a fleet designed to keep the conduits clear of snow, ice and salt, while others left the task to road vehicles or by equipping passenger or works cars with snow ploughs. Leeds had five purpose-made snow sweepers of the American JG Brill design, but none survived into the preservation era. When the opportunity came to purchase one of the similar snow broom cars, originally from Brussels, this was taken up and their No. 96 came to Crich where it was smartened up for display in the Exhibition Hall. Number 96 is a genuine Brill example, dating from 1906, although Brussels seems to have plundered the Brill design and used this as a template for vehicles they built for themselves.

Should No.96 ever be required for use, it would be of little help in the Derbyshire winters as, in its present configuration for Continental running, if run in normal service between other service cars it would simply push all the cleared snow on to the other track!

PLAYING AWAY

Edinburgh 35, facing, Blackpool 4, above, Manchester 765 and Hill of Howth 10 below, all in Blackpool for the 1985 Centenary Celebrations. Derek Shepherd, who masterminded No.4's reincarnation, is at the helm, above, in Lytham Road, returning to Rigby Road depot.

PLAYING AWAY

Cunarder 1297 at the Glasgow Garden Festival, 1988.

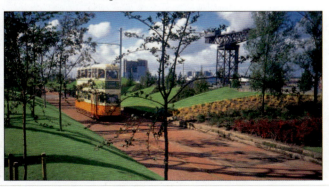

Newcastle 102 at the Gateshead Garden Festival in 1990, carrying a typically good load, and below, also at Gateshead, with Blackpool 167.

MISCELLANY

To avoid unhitching horses at each terminal, and to reduce the weight of a second staircase and the associated space, some systems adopted the Eades Patent reversible truck. This allowed the bodywork to be released from its securing mechanism, and swivelled round through 180º, being pulled round by the horses. The National Tramway Museum was fortunate in being able to obtain a truck of this type from the remains of a tram once used by the Manchester Carriage and Tramways Company, a large user of the type. It has still to be restored, but inspection reveals exactly how it worked.

Another Eades truck of the same type has been restored in Manchester, complete with reconstructed double-deck bodywork with 'garden seats' on the upper-deck as above, as part of the Heaton Park collection. This is the only example of a complete Eades car, and will be on display in Manchester to commemorate its 130th anniversary of introduction into service in 1877.

There are three unrestored horse car bodies in the Crich collection, some of which can be seen in the Museum. These comprise an example of an Eades car as shown above, together with conventional examples (*ie* non-reversible) from the London Tramway Company dating from 1895 and number 1 from the Warwick & Leamington system.

FUTURE PROJECTS

Visitors to the Crich Tramway Village can see trams in varying stages of preservation. These range from the semi-derelict, to the active restoration in the workshops and the fully operational fleet. Not all of the collection is housed at Crich, and the exhibits are moved around from time-to-time to make way for imported examples as they take their place in the workshops. Due to the skills required, the fact that many parts have to be made from scratch, and the costs that these imply, no proper restoration can be done on the cheap or hurried. They tend to take around two years, although much depends on the condition of the tram being dealt with.

Currently there are two trams at the Museum undergoing restoration but awaiting completion; London United Tramways No. 159 and Blackpool Railcoach No. 298. Others will follow, and the contenders include the Cardiff Water Car No. 131, hopefully for 2009 to mark the 50th anniversary of its arrival as the first tram at Crich. Pressure is building for London Transport No. 1 (The London County Council tramways' swansong) and Blackpool 'Dreadnought' No. 59 also to undergo thorough restoration. All of these trams have been illustrated in earlier pages.

In addition, there are a number of potential future exhibits including a four-wheel balcony double-decker from Nottingham Corporation Tramways, their number 166, and a coal tram from Oporto, Portugal. Who knows what other aspirants may still lie undetected?

Often when hulks arrive for rebuilding, photographs alone are insufficient to portray completely the finished result. Fortunately, skilled model makers can often fill the gap as can be seen below with a model of London 159.

ON THE MOVE

Out Rawcliffe 4¼
Pilling 8¼
Knott End 11½

One question crops up more than all the others when visitors look round the Museum – how on earth do you get these trams into this space? Well, here's the answer. It looks easy , but consider the cost of hiring the special rig and planning out routes that avoid low bridges (thus often precluding the use of motorways when moving double-deckers). Then there is the need to arrange the discreet police escort following at a safe distance to keep errant motorists in check. In the earliest days it was also necessary to hire heavy lifting cranes at each end of the journey but nowadays roll-on-roll-off techniques are mercifully employed.

This Glasgow tram has led a busy life since 1962 when its working days finished and it made the long journey to Crich. It was one of the stars of the 1985 Blackpool Centenary events and it was back in Glasgow for the duration of the1988 Garden Festival.

In the view above, Knott End will be familiar to those who know Fleetwood, being just across the Wyre Estuary, and accessed by a ferry from the well-known tram terminus. It should be mentioned that moving trams on main roads such as this is, of course, a very different challenge to that of negotiating country lanes around Crich!

GONE BUT NOT FORGOTTEN

As one part of the celebrations for the closure of the Sheffield system, their stores car 349 was specially painted and fitted-up with coloured lights. When this duty was done, the car came to Crich, and formed the basis of the first TMS generator car. Part of the side was removed to allow a Gardner diesel engine and generator to be installed in the saloon.

Re-numbered '01', the car could propel itself and feed power into the overhead line for others.

It fell out of use when static plant was installed, and parts were salvaged for future use, principally the truck which is now fitted to Chesterfield No. 7.

It is seen, above, in Sheffield, before the final procession began, and below, on the siding at Crich which became its home for some time. Newly-arrived Glasgow 22 can be seen receiving some attention in the background.

ACKNOWLEDGEMENTS

The compilers wish to thank all their fellow members who, over the last fifty years, have helped them enjoy working in the development of the Museum. The illustrations in this handbook speak volumes as to what has been achieved, but one thing which struck us both as we came into the Museum for the 50th Anniversary Celebrations in 2005 was the wonderful profusion of trees and shrubs, putting the trams back into some of the sylvan locations of bygone days. We would particularly thank Geoffrey Claydon for his kind advice, and also Mike Crabtree and his colleagues in the Tramcar Workshop for checking the accuracy of the details concerning the trams themselves. The view below ought to be savoured by everyone who visits the National Tramway Museum – it was taken from the gallery overlooking the workshop area and is readily accessible by stairs or a lift. It demonstrates some of the behind-the-scenes activities, and really should not be missed.